LIFE
in
DARKNESS

RITIK SHUKLA

First Published in November 2021

ISBN: 978-93-5472-679-8

BLUEROSE PUBLISHERS

www.bluerosepublishers.com

info@bluerosepublishers.com

+91 8882 898 898

Cover Design:

Aveek

Typographic Design:

Namrata Saini

Distributed by: BlueRose, Amazon, Flipkart, Shopclues

PREFACE

As we all know, people are fond of good poetry, and all of us like to share or express our feelings and thoughts that are being cultivated in our mind. So, this book will provide you everything that you wanted to express for someone using word play. You might get overwhelmed while reading and being involved with the feelings this book has been written. You will find a story or your feelings somewhere in this book. So focus and enjoy the journey of words.

ABOUT THE POET

RITIK SHUKLA

Date of Birth; July, 10, 2003

Place of Birth; Fatehpur, Uttar Pradesh

Ritik Shukla was born on July 10, 2003, in a village named Datauli, Fatehpur, U.P. He went to his grandfather's home in Banda when he was 6 years old, for his studies. He was there for 7 years, till the year 2014. After completing his primary education, he came back to his parents at Kanpur and has been continuing his studies there. When he was 12, he wrote his first poem for his mother, thinking about her while she was not with him. When he came to Kanpur he started writing poems in Hindi and English. With the help of his English teacher, Mr. Nehal Nigam, he started writing more. He passed out of class 10 in the year 2019 and, 3 months later, he completed a 100 poems in both the languages. He decided to mould his thoughts into the shape of a book. He has now successfully completed two books – Life in Darkness(English) and Mehek (Hindi).

ACKNOWLEDGEMENT

I'm feeling privileged to thank my loved ones. First of all, I would like to thank my parents who always supported me with everything that's required.

Then my aunt, Mrs. Shrddha Tiwari, for being with me all the time and being my inspiration during the time I was writing.

My English teacher, Mr. Nehal Nigam, and Mr. Ranjeet Kushwaha for giving me linguistic knowledge, and Mr. Umesh Singh for helping me throughout by creating content for publishing.

My publishers, Bluerose Publication, for trusting me and my content, and supporting me with my projects.

A bad day never implies you have a bad life. it's you and your thoughts which make you feel bad.

- Ritik shukla

Wishing you all a very happy and joyful reading journey.

POEM-1

It's been 2 months since you left
and I think about you every day.
Whenever I get lonely
I remember what you used to say.
Never have I loved someone
as much as I love you,
and even though you hurt me
my feelings will always remain true.
I have so much to ask you,
so much I want to say:
Why did you leave me?
Why did things end up this way?
I think back to the last day I saw you
and the hurt that was in your eyes;
I never once thought
that would be our goodbyes.
If there was anything I could take back,
it would be the lonely nights
and my selfish ways.
Maybe instead of writing this, I would be holding you tight.

POEM-2

Can we just run away?
Together, just me and you.
Have fun, forever play—
you know, just the two of us.
Can we just leave this place?
Just run hand-in-hand,
be together all our days
and never ever look back.
Can we just walk?
Together under the stars;
I'll kiss your hand and your lips,
and you can have my heart.
Can we just laugh?
Innocent giggles, loving looks;
I'll have your love and you can have mine
because it's my heart and love you took.
Can we just walk?
for hours on end;
we'll talk about anything
and we can lay upon your bed.

POEM-3

Everything was simple,
everything was fine.
I knew I couldn't have you
and I knew why.
I tried to move on,
I dated other guys.
But then when we'd hang out
I knew I had lied to myself.
You noticed me drifting.
You said, "Please explain."
But I didn't want to lose you,
so I tried to deal with the pain.
It's hard to be with you,
it gets harder each day.
When I look into your eyes,
I feel my body floating away.
I miss the way it used to be.
You don't feel the change;
you don't know I really love you.
I'm sure to you it's just a game.
As I close my eyes tonight,
I'll pray as I was taught to do;
I'll pray that you realize that
I love you but I can't have you.

POEM-4

I’m going where the rainbows glow
and the clouds will never cry,
the sun will sit upon the earth
to warm the heavens with its shine;
where the sweetest scent of the roses
will be carried with the breeze,
to mingle with the garden fruits,
the butterflies, and the bees.
The birds will sing together,
and the nights will all be day.
The stars will forever twinkle,
and the flowers will never fade;
so this is where you will find me
when my time on earth is done.
I’ll go to be in the great heaven
with all of God’s chosen ones.

POEM-5

You say you are my friend,
but you stab me in the back.
I sit here in my blood,
wondering if you will ever come back.
And as I suffer,
the days go by.
I'm wondering what this is;
why do I feel so dry?
We once used to be happy,
but now it's all disappeared.
This feeling of pressure
is slowly getting near.
My suffering increasing
as the days go by,
and I'm sitting here wondering
why you said goodbye.

POEM-6

God's love sets me free—
this is my victory song.
His grace is sufficient for me,
it is what keeps me strong,
for I'm no perfect man
and on my own cannot prevail.
Sometimes, doing the best I can,
evil will come to no avail.

Had my share of heartaches,
sometimes wondering to what end;
made my share of mistakes—
over this, I can't pretend.
The struggle may increase
but it's no cause for alarm.
God's thoughts to me are of peace,
to nurture and not to harm.

I force on quite resolved
gods at work in me for the best.
I'm flawed but fiercely loved,
and he is not finished yet.
God's perfect plan for me,
I may not fully understand.
But trusting, obeying, I'm grateful to be
handled in his loving hand.

POEM-7

Hear my cries! I need your help;
please come save me from myself.

Be my friend, a guiding light,
give me strength to do what's right.

Find my heart, I've lost my way...
Tell me I will be okay.

Feel my pain and catch my tears,
help me conquer all these fears.

Let my silence speak to you.
Find some way to help me through.

Put yourself into my shoes,
and just like me, you'll be confused.

POEM-8

Of course I'm fine, why do you ask?
Oh, don't mind this, it's just my mask:
it hides the grief, it hides the strife,
I wear this mask to escape the knife.

Don't forget this, my pain is real
I'm not lying, this is how I feel.
You sit there saying it can't be true;
it is for me, just not for you.

You say my heart must be a sight,
gold as ice and black as night.
It's not my heart, only my soul,
but killing me must be your goal.

You're getting close, I hope you know
you really don't have far to go.
Soon enough I'll reach my end,
you'll have my soul to tear and rend.

But you don't know, you never ask,
you never look beyond the mask.
The look on my face is giving me away
I wonder now, what will you say?

You've asked me here, you'll know now
I'll take it off, I'll take a bow.
I can't do it now, tell you the truth
I must keep up my pretense of youth.

"Of course I'm fine, why do you ask?
Oh, don't mind this, it's just my mask."

POEM-9

The sun went away,
the sky went black,
up came the wind
I feel on my back.

It started to run,
I began to sink,
then I lifted my head
and took a drink.

I perked myself up
and said, "Please don't cry,"
and wiped off my petals
until they were dry.

The cloud soon parted
and out came the sun.
The beauty in me
has only begun.

POEM-10

The earth is stained with human anguish,
by such infamous deeds we can't dismiss.
Why should we all die in terrible torment,
or be stuck down at any unjust moment?

With our beautiful cities lying waste in ashes,
when the army's of the powers embrace in clashes,
while the horn of the oppressor is blown
and the seeds of destruction are sown;

It is for the eyes of the world to find every fault,
and to correct them before our civilization in naught.
What good is it to say that victory was mine
when, in doing so, I served every family line.

Blacks, and whites, and all shades between,
know we're heading for more conflicts then there's ever been.
And how will we receive Christ when we return to earth again?
Will he be nailed to a cross once more by us?

POEM-11

Have you ever had the feeling
you were meant for something great,
but you just couldn't find it?
Maybe it could be too late,
you can feel it in your heart;
it tells you to keep on trying
because a life without this gift
is pointless, there's no denying.

Like a sprinkle of magic
falling from the sky,
and you keep on asking:
is this really mine?
The world tries to take it away,
as sure as the sun will rise,
but it shines within who you are,
locked away within your eyes.

Without the help of you,
this gift will have no power.
Like a tool in the toolbox
or the minute in the hour,
a world without writing
is destined to be tragic.
But it's the world in the writer
that truly holds the magic.

POEM-12

There is more to poetry
than rhythm and rhyme:
it's a window to our souls,
undiminished by time;

It's where tears and joys
are clearly expressed;
it's the thoughts that ordinarily
might be repressed;

It can be set to music,
increasing it's worth,
sending joy to the heavens
that encompass the earth.

You can make almost anything
become immortal
by poetic words
sent over the portals.

So put down your thoughts
when you have inspiration,
you'll be adding your part
to the whole of creations.

POEM-13

Our habit has always been
to seek support,
getting it from anyone
who can afford,
also from your family
living in the abode,

Giving us happiness
and better grip and hold;
those who support others,
they are like gold,
providing warmth to those
who are stuck in cold.
Taking it easy
and the concept is old,
so learn to give support
and always be bold.

POEM-14

Hanging from the vine were
bunches of grapes ripe,
all full of sweet juice,
none was of sour type.

Tempted underneath was
a watching greedy fox;
she tried to jump to grapes,
but they were far off.

Decrying the grapes, she
left the place in haste
saying, all grapes are sour
not even worthy to taste.

Never do thou, O' children,
speak ill of others;
ever tried the path of truth
even in the odd hours.

POEM-15

Get out of the bed!
Sunshine's getting red;
glory of the day break
is reflected in the lake.

Birds are all out of nest,
nature is at its best,
atmosphere all is gay,
shining with each sun ray.
In the fields, green crops
to up keep the eye sight,
grass green is ever right.

Cool breeze of early hours
gives body healthy showers.
Breathing in the open air
works as a natural care.

POEM-16

The fisherman goes out at dawn
when everyone's abed,
and from the bottom of the sea,
draws up his daily bread.

His life is strange; half on the shore
and half upon the sea,
not quite a fish, and yet not quite
the same as you and me.

The fisherman has curious eyes;
they make you feel so queer,
as if they had seen many things
of wonder, and of fear.

They're like the sea on foggy days—
not gray, not yet quite blue;
they're like the wondrous tales he tells
not quite – yet maybe – true.

He knows so much of boats and tides,
of winds and clouds and sky!
But when I tell of city things,
he sniffs and shuts one eye.

POEM-17

How good to lie a little while
and look up through the tree!
The sky is like a kind big smile
bent sweetly over me.

The sunshine flickers through the lace
of leaves above my head,
and kisses me upon the face
like mother, before bed.

The wind comes stealing o'er the grass
to whisper pretty things,
and though I cannot see him pass,
I feel his careful wings.

So many gentle friends are near
whom one can scarcely see,
a child should never feel a fear,
wherever he may be.

POEM-18

No one can tell me,
nobody knows,
where the wind comes from,
where the wind goes.

It's flying from somewhere
as fast as it can,
I couldn't keep up with it,
not if I ran.

But if I stopped holding
the string of my kite,
it would blow with the wind
for a day and a night.

And then when I found it,
Wherever it blew,
I should know that the wind
had been going there too.

So then I could tell them
where the wind goes…
but where the wind comes from,
nobody knows.

POEM-19

The moon has a face like
the clock in the wall;
she shines on thieves
on the garden wall,
on streets and fields and harbor quays,
and birdies asleep in the forks of the trees.

The squalling cat and the squeaking mouse,
the howling dog by the door of the house,
the bat that lies in the bed at noon,
all love to be out by the light of the moon.

But all the things
that belong to the day,
cuddle to sleep
to be out of her way;
and flowers and children close their eyes
till up in the morning the sun shall arise.

POEM-20

As the ocean waves at me
and the sand greets the sea,
the fish swims free,
and shells wash up by me.

The sand squishes suddenly
between my shoeless toes,
then the tide flows over them
and back down it goes.

The salt is on my tongue,
the sea's song is sung,
the sun is going down,
and so my day at sea is done.

POEM-21

Waves come crashing to grey sullen shores;
powerful and strong, it breathes and roars.
Cascading and caressing each grain of sand,
a warm embrace between sea and land.

High above, a seagull soars high;
wings of purity, it spreads to fly.
Battling high against darkened cloud,
in a wind that blows fiercely, flying graceful and proud.

Beneath, the sand is soft and warm,
sculpted by nature, it's weathered the storm.
A passionate battle between calmness and rage,
A new chapter's beginning—don't turn the last page.

I listen again to the whispering waves,
music of nature, calming and brave.
Its power unknown, its stillness untamed,
mysterious and magical, a treasure earth claims.

POEM-22

I never imagined myself to be
that guy who falls so hard in love,
just to land with two broken parts
of a whole, which is now just a broken heart.

I see now how insane it was loving you,
like the stars hold the moon and all that crap;
the voices, the cries, the blue bright veins,
I realize now that this was all just a game.

I look in the mirror and I don't see myself,
I see what you made me, a creature from hell;
you never even saw a single tear fall,
cause I kept my walls high to hide it all.

But still, here I am,
wondering whether I should forget you or not,
wondering whether I should pull the trigger or not.

POEM-23

Today, crossing that white bench again,
I walked down the memory lane of pain.
This is the place where my 'love story' begins.
And the memories flashed where I
was sitting with you, holding your hands;
not caring about the time, if it was
day or dawn,
I witnessed here with you several
winters, summers, and rain.
And one day you came saying I am
moving on as there is no gain.
I cried and gave several reasons to
why should we retain,
but you were departed and I was in deep strain.
I sat here several days so that I can attain
that my love was not so volatile and
I did not complain,
The pretty pink flowers next to the
bench helped me contain.
My love is pure and I trust I will meet
the 'one' who really deserves it;
this is my faith, my belief about
which I am so certain.

POEM-24

You pushed me into the corner
with no hole to escape
and, like a psycho, you left.

You made me insecure,
tried to manipulate me,
demolished my self confidence.

Why do you have to be so rude?
I know the world is crude,
but secretly dare you post my nude.

Having you gone may be
was a blessing in disguise,
it really was good riddance.

I hope you go die
excruciating with pain,
agonized with memories,
tortured till death,
just like I;
this is my goodbye.

POEM-25

Looking through the window,
there is a small child
sitting with his pillow;
he has been there for a while.

He is nervous about the room
and the place where he stands,
his smile turned to gloom
when he sees my large hands.

Looking deeper through the pane
to see what is wrong,
he's not sure he is sane,
he has been there way too long

As I peer into the glass,
the child starts to fade,
leaving no mass,
and me standing in the shade.

POEM-26

I want to change the world.
I want to impact it so deep
that I reach the core.
I want to change the meaning of peace
to something permanent.
I want to open doors
and shut out doubts.
I want the past to dissolve;
it makes my ears bleed,
mistakes linked in memory,
time's so hard the world shakes in its boots.

I want to change the world.
The sun rises and then sets,
but leaves its mark before it goes,
it creates life and growth.
The moon brings serenity and mystery
—Both bring death too.
I want the growth to shine through
but erase the death.
I want to change the world
but I would not dare change the past.

POEM-27

Don't be worried about the past,
things like that never last.
We're better than yesterday,
we never run out of things to say.

If you were strong yesterday,
you're strong every day.
The past makes us stronger,
it does not make us weaker.

The past make us realize
that we're better than this.
The past is just a time
but it is never being missed.

POEM-28

My life is changing,
the life that I've had,
it's changing forever
but no need to be sad.

It's time to move on,
time to start anew,
I jumped from the nest
with some trouble, I flew.

I might hit a few bumps,
maybe make a wrong turn,
but all of those troubles are lessons I'll learn.

So as my life changes
I hope that you'll see,
it's you who I'll credit
for the life that I lead.

POEM-29

Fumbling, stumbling
around in the dark.
Fighting, igniting
flames from a spark.

Blinded, reminded
of the fear inside.
Turning, yearning
for a place to hide.

Soaking, choking,
struggling to breathe.
Hiding, abiding,
my ghost won't leave.

Chasing, racing,
I stagger away.
Breathless, restless,
in the mud I lay.

Dreaming, gleaming,
I escape the past.
Winning, new beginning,
I am free at last.

POEM-30

I will never take for granted
how greatly I've been blessed
for when it comes to parents—
mom and dad, you're the best!

You nurtured and protected me,
and taught me with great care.
And every time I've needed you,
you were always there.

If you could look into my heart,
how quickly you would see,
the special place you hold there
and how much you mean to me.

May you receive the blessings
you are so deserving of,
for your caring and sharing,
and each sacrifice of love.

And may you carry in your hearts
these words forever true…
No parents anywhere on earth
could be loved more than you.

POEM-31

There was a time you held my hand;
you gave me strength to stand.

When I would cry and be up all night,
you would cuddle me, spend sleepless nights.

And the next, when I slept all day,
you tried hard to buy me toys.

So I thank you mama, and I thank you papa,
for giving me this beautiful life.

I have been wrong, and I have been lost,
but you have stood by me and shown me the path.

I have asked for things, those which I need not,
you gave them all to me, just to see my smile.

Oceans so deep, mountains so high,
can't express my feelings for you;
You have been my mentor, you have made me what I am.

POEM-32

When I was hopeless, you were there;
You picked me up, you showed me care.
Without the love you had for me,
god only knows where I would be.

To me, you were a second mom:
a person I drew wisdom from.
In my corner every fight,
you always cared that things were right.

I won't forget the things you've done,
I felt like your adopted son.
Ready now and feeling new,
I couldn't leave not thanking you.

POEM-33

You're a very special person.
I'm glad that you're my friend,
for when I need a little advice,
you always have some to lend.

You help me when I am troubled,
feeling down and out.
I never have to say what's wrong,
you seem to know what I'm all about.

I can always tell my feelings
without having you put me down;
you're the person I can turn to
when no one else is around.

I can cry on your shoulders
when things are going wrong.
You give me a smile
and help me to be strong.

You seem to understand me
after all that we've gone through,
I only have one thing to say…
Thanks for being you!

POEM-34

We have been friends for not so long,
we've learned to trust and share a song.
We used to laugh and used to cry,
we've been together and learned to fly.

Those sweet memories we both have shared,
I will always treasure, I will always care,
for all those moments we've been together
are oh so precious! more precious than jasper.

I wish no worship and pains arrive
that block this feeling and forever deprive,
for if I lose the inspiration you've shared,
my heart in agony forever will suffer.

With all my hearts, I do sincerely pray
that this precious friendship forever will stay.
Deep in my soul, a vow I will offer:
you'll always be my friend, from now until forever.

POEM-35

You think you're so good,
think you're so perfect in everything,
you think you can control my mood;
please, you must be joking.

I gave you all my heart,
I believed in everything you would say.
I trusted you from the start,
and everything went your way.

I guess I made my biggest mistake
when I became loyal to you.
You're one of those friends who is fake
in everything you say and do.

I thought your kindness would last,
but now I feel so used,
because when I think of the past,
I thought you'd never give my heart a bruise.

Why did I ever rely on a word you said?
What did I ever do to deserve this pain?
I trusted you, but you hurt me instead,
and I don't know if I could believe you again.

POEM-36

Farewell words too often part
and cleave with sorrow to aching hearts.
With a final wave, all disappears
beneath the hush of silent tears.

Why can't sorrow be as kind
as to hide away and stay confined?
And leave us only thoughts of bliss,
of joyful things to reminisce.

So focus not on sorrows, born
where happy times are now forlorn,
but instead of joy and merriment
and delight all felt without relent.

And with all the love to fill our hearts,
sorrow and pain then soon departs.
And although goodbyes are bittersweet,
we can no longer feel incomplete.

POEM-37

Best friends are angels
that god sent along.
They always stay beside you
whenever things go wrong.

I'm glad that god blessed me,
with a good friend such as you.
A person to be there,
a person to get me through.

Never turn away from me,
I can't bear to be apart.
All the pain and suffering
will be too much for my heart.

You are my best friend,
the one who brightens my day,
the one who cheers me up,
the one who's here to stay.

POEM-38

I met you as a stranger. Then picked you as my friend.
Our friendship is something that will never end.
When I was in darkness that needed some light,
you came to me and hugged me tight.

You took my hands and dried my tears,
you woke me up to end my fears.
You took my hand and made me see,
that God has a special plan for me.

You helped me laugh,
when I was sad.
You made me tough,
when I felt bad.

Our friendship made me see the light,
our friendship showed me what was right.
I hope our friendship will never bend.
I hope our friendship will never end.

POEM-39

I hate the snow, I hate the sleet,
I just want some rain.
The clouds are running across the sky,
playing some silly game.

It's already spring,
and the snow is still piling,
that's why the birds can't sing,
and why the sky isn't sky.

Out of all the towns,
why did Jack Frost pick this one?
To send chilling winds,
and abandon the sun?

It really is very cold,
and the heater is always on.
The indoor plants are growing mold,
it's freezing from dusk till dawn.

I wish that I could be anywhere but here,
it's like a cold he—from sky,
I've had enough of it, it better change,
or I fear that I will die.

POEM-40

The joke was very funny,
she laughed a lot of tears,
when suddenly her eye fell out
and landed in her beer.
She fished around with her pudding spoon
but it just stared back,
through the beery gloom.
She tried again with her fountain pen,
but she only saw it
now and then.
What to do, she tried to decide,
pondered and pondered,
sighed and sighed.
In a fit of madness,
she downed her drink,
swallowed her eye,
with not even a blink.
She rang her doctor in a fit of remorse,
who simply advised her,
"Let nature take its course."
I believe she's still waiting, it's playing hide and seek.
So she's had to buy another eye,
to see her through the week.

POEM-41

It seemed like a good idea at the time,
but looking back now I cringe just a little.
I was so hungry and it was once mine,
the week-old milk and peanut butter brittle.

It wasn't just the smell,
no, it was something much worse.
Yes I had nothing to rid me of
this unquenchable thirst.

The crust was thick and the color was off,
the smell was foul and made me cough.
Not before long, the stench filled the air.
What's that? Oh goodness, do I see a hair?

Now wait just a minute, that isn't fair.
Oh please, I'm so hungry, what else is there?
I looked in the pantry and I looked in fridge,
I'll go to the store sooner or later.

The most horrible snack,
when nothing to eat,
I admit it, I did it,
I ate the gross treat.

POEM-42

She stood there by the ocean,
the breeze gently lifted her hair.
Of that seagull just above her,
she was totally unaware.

Seemingly floating in the sky,
the seagull's wings were still.
I think it paused to take good aim,
and drop a mess at will.

Too late she looked above her head,
when the seagull hovered now.
Then, as I watched in horror,
bird dropping hit her brow.

Her scream pierced the balmy air,
splat! The stuff hit her face.
Then she saw my camera and me,
and stomped off in disgrace.

POEM-43

I did not wish to write this poem,
but it would not leave me be.
Throughout the night,
throughout the day,
no matter what, it wouldn't go away.

I did not wish to write this poem,
but it took over me.
Forced my hand to pen it down,
my brain to think of nothing else.
Until it was done, I knew no rest.

I did not wish to write this poem,
but here it is before me.
The ghost that proposed me laid to rest;
these last lines are the final rites,
for the poem I did not wish to write.

POEM-44

The bulls of Bickerton Lane do graze
upon my verdant lawn.
I hear them in the morning haze,
mooing to the dawn.

They trample all my flowered shrubs,
they crush the dainty rose,
and then they pee this giant stream
as from a garden hose.

And what's this sticking to my shoe?
'Tis this I truly hate.
For it's the sticking residue
of what the beasties ate.

So then I say, let's have some fun.
We'll let them eat the grass.
Whilst with my trusty BB gun,
I shoot them in the ass!

POEM-45

So now he has had his eyes done,
and at last he can see.
But I was bit worried—
What would he think of me?

You see, he hadn't seen me,
out of two good eyes.
Would I be a total shock,
or a nice surprise?

He said, "My god, you are almost grey,
your eyes are much too small.
You are old and fat and ugly,
I'm not impressed at all!"

But as I sat there crying,
I suddenly noticed that—
he wasn't looking my way,
but talking to the cat!

So, yes, I think he's very pleased
with all that he can see.
He thinks everything is so lovely,
and that includes me!

POEM-46

What's with this daylight saving time?
It steals our sleeping, snoozing time;
roll out of bed and a breath,
and feels like microwave-reheated death.

Seven o'clock? That just can't be,
it's way too dark out there to see.
Coffee? Yes, I need two cups
to get my sluggish body up.

And hit the road before the sun,
for Monday's way-too-early "fun".
It's lunchtime? Huh? I just got here!
My head is just now barely clear.

Afternoon meeting? How can that be?
I thought it was one...how is it three?
The end of day has almost come,
The day flew by...it's almost done!

Five o'clock, well that's fine!
I like this daylight savings time!

POEM-47

As I lay cozy, all snug in my bed,
I enjoy the imagination inside my head,
until I hear a racket beside my bed—
it's my 5am alarm!

I quickly silence you, you annoying alarm,
then we snooze together and let
dreams carry on.
Enjoying the peace, then I'll be darned;
it's my 5.15 reminder!

Now I hush the ringing of my reminder,
OK alarm, let's put that behind us.
Eyes just shut, but here goes that timer—
it's 7.20, I'm late!

POEM-48

He says he's leaving,
he'll be gone about a year.
He's headed off to fight the war,
and his time is drawing near.
I have no words of wisdom,
to ease our aching hearts.
He'll be gone and I'll be here,
a thousand miles apart.
The danger that soldiers face,
he knows it all too well.
Still, he keeps our spirits up,
as our throats begin to swell.
The morning comes all too fast;
I'm not prepared at all.
Because I know there is a chance,
my soldier won't come home.
My soldier is a strong man,
one that's brave and true.
He's not afraid of dying;
he flights for me and you.
So, if you see a soldier,
give him lots of praise.
Tell him that you are thankful;
you see the price we pay.

POEM-49

Mary had a little lamb,
and a baked potato.
Mary had a salad too,
of lettuce and tomato.

Mary asked for wine to drink,
so daddy poured her some.
But mommy said, "If you drink that,
I'll whip your little bum!"

So Mary chose dessert instead;
she had a choice to make:
should I have a slice of pie,
or a piece of cake?

But Mary couldn't quite decide,
so she took a bite of each.
It seemed the pie was rancid plum,
and the cake was rotted peach.

She gagged and spat the gross stuff out,
and hurled on the floor.
'Twas then her mother grabbed her hair
and threw her out the door.

POEM-50

Green is so important
because we see it all around,
it's up very high on the trees,
and on the grass that's on the ground.

Green is the color of
the plants that grow in the south,
it's also the color of brussels sprouts,
that I refuse to put in my mouth.

Green is on the traffic light
when the cars can go.
All the green disappears
when it starts to snow.

The important thing about the color green
is because of my mother;
No, she is not green,
it's her favorite color.

POEM-51

You hear of true love in movies and books,
but not based on popularity or looks.
I've searched every corner deep in my mind,
but this one little thing, I just could not find;

for it was not in my head, but in my heart,
looking for this completely tore me apart.
Then one day I found it, this thing we call love,
it's something wonderful, sent from above.

We stared at each other as our faces turned red,
yet nothing was spoken, nothing was said.
No words were needed, because our heart said all,
we'd be together forever, for in love we did fall.

POEM-52

To you, I give the whole me,
for I believe that you're my destiny.
To you, I offer every best of my heart,
for I believe that you will value it.

I want to share my whole life with you,
for me to show that my love is true.
I want to hold you in my arms,
and sing you songs and lullabies.

Loving you is what I want to do,
although I know that it can make me blue.
'Cause tears in my eyes have nothing to do,
if I'm with a man that is you.

POEM-53

Orange and pink shoot across the sky,
I can see it from where I lie;
the sun is setting, going to sleep,
the dark surrounds, like the ocean deep.

The stars come, twinkling lights;
glittering diamonds, what a sight.
I lie in the grass and up I stare,
my body goes numb as I forget all my cares.

I like to gaze up at the stars,
so I can forget my cares and all my scars.

I have no one to look after me,
the real me is someone no one can see.
So I'll wait until I find some sort of love,
and until then it's just me and the stars above.

POEM-54

I've never imagined that there can be this day,
a day that love will find its way
out of my heart and into your soul,
these feelings I have are beyond my control.

All my life, I have waited patiently,
for a goddess like you, so beautiful, so lovely.
Words can't express the way I feel;
these feelings towards you are all for real.

You are the reason why I go on,
eternity can't separate this special bond.
This heart of mine is reserved for you,
forever it is yours, this love is true.

I'll be your first and you'll be my last;
my world, my everything, till my time has past.
I will always love you until the end of time,
my Love, my Sweetheart, my Valentine.

POEM-55

When I am looking into your eyes,
I see all the love you have for me;
I see in your eyes you care for me a lot.
I see your love for me is true,
and you'll do whatever it takes to have me in your eyes.

When I am looking into your eyes,
I see your love for me is unconditional.
Your eyes tell me you will never leave me,
you will always stay by my side
to protect and cherish me.

When I am looking into your eyes,
I see with you everything is possible.
I see in your eyes your love for me is everlasting.
Your eyes tell me you really, really love me.

POEM-56

I haven't written a poem
since the last time I was hurt.
I haven't written a poem
since my heart was ready to burst.
But now you got me writing,
not because I'm sad;
now you got me writing
about things I never had.
I never had someone call me
and tell me they care for me.
I never had anyone
just stop and stare at me,
And tell me that I'm sexy,
and tell me to never be sad.
I've written you these poems,
so you would know how I feel.
I want you to know I want you,
and I want you to know I'm real.

POEM-57

Wondering why you have so much hate.
Before you see, it will be too late.
Trying to accept who you are
just seems far too far.

All the pain that you have created,
just sits within you with so much hatred.
Hoping you will come to see
what everyone else seems to believe.

All I want is for you to realize,
you're burning bridges with the one who tries.
Open your heart and let me in
before I just give up, let it end.

It will take years to fix these issues,
I just hope by then I can still trust you.
How much more do you think I can take?
You won't see until it's too late.

POEM-58

It's that look in your eye,
it's the smile on your face,
that makes time slip by
and I know I'm in a better place.

It's the memories of you I have
that make any grey sky turn blue,
and let me know these feelings
I have are true.

Getting lost in my dreams
with the mere image of you,
it's hard to imagine; it seems
a future lost, one without you.

So I leave my arms open,
and I'll wish and may pray,
eyes focused and hoping,
for your embrace, just one more day.

POEM-59

Who will cry for the little girl?
A little girl, is she.
Who will cry for the little girl?
The one with the broken home.
Who will cry for the little girl?
A good girl, is she.
Who will cry for the little girl?
The one who hurts so bad.
Who will cry for the little girl?
So scared to grow up.
Who will cry for the little girl?
Lost and confused.
Who will cry for the little girl?
Who does not understand?
Who will cry for her?
I'll cry for that little girl.
Who is scared and misunderstood?
Who will cry for the little girl too?

POEM-60

This day I will never forget,
the moment when we first met.
At the balcony, I saw you once,
a beautiful sight, though seen at one glance.

I will never forget that beautiful sight,
a beautiful girl, behind her: the sunlight.
That moment kept my world from turning,
that moment kept my heart from beating.

But the time seems to go too fast,
this moment never seems to last.
But in my memories this'll be kept forever,
until the time that we'll be together.

That day I will never forget,
a beautiful girl, behind her: the sunset.
That day my love for you was so true,
kept in my heart, my one and only you.

POEM-61

I never really knew you,
you were just another friend.
But when I got to know you,
I let my heart unbend.

I couldn't help past memories,
which would make me cry.
I had to forget my first love
and give another try.

So I've fallen in love with you,
and I'll never let you go.
I love you more than anyone,
I just had to let you know.

My feelings for you will never change,
just know my feelings are true,
just remember this one thing,
I will always love you.

POEM-62

My smile hides my tears,
my laugh hides my screams;
it's been this way for years,
things aren't as they seem.

I always seem so happy,
with not a care in the world.
But you should know, sadly,
many things go untold.

Nobody really knows me,
they only know my cover.
But I wish I could let it free,
let them know what's under.

But instead, I practice
my smiles in the mirror.
Then the next thing I do is,
make my fake laugh clearer.

What is wrong? You need help?
Is all they will ask,
So I have decided,
to live behind a mask.

POEM-63

Laid my head upon your chest,
your arms encircled me;
it was, my love, as if we were
what God meant us to be.

I closed my eyes and heard your heart,
your soft smile in my hair.
I'd never felt so whole and safe,
our hearts beating as a pair.

You found my eyes and told me of
a love for me, undying.
I kissed your face and knew right then,
it was in Heaven we were lying.

POEM-64

The grass so green,
the sun so bright.
Life seems a dream,
no worries in sight.

Tans and tank tops,
laughter and bliss.
Each moment passes,
without even a miss.

Friends and cookouts,
memories and laughs.
Good times to remember,
but how long will it last?

The grass soon fades,
leaves begin to fall.
School replaces sleepovers,
oh, I'll miss it all.

POEM-65

In your arms, you hold me tight,
never letting go through the night.
All my dreams are peaceful because of you,
holding me in your arms like you do.

Your lips are as sweet as ever;
I wish to kiss them forever.
My heart beats only for you,
holding me in your arms like you do.

When we met, I knew it was fate,
I found my one true soul mate.
As I look into your loving eyes,
knowing our love will never die.

So hold me in your warm embrace,
in your arms, I'll be no other place.
To be with the one I love, which is you,
holding me in your arms like you do.

POEM-66

I want to run, I want to hide,
from all the pain she caused inside.
I want to scream, I want to cry;
why can't I tell her goodbye?

I want to move on; I just can't let go.
I love her more than she will ever know.
I want to start over, I want to feel free!
But this pain will never leave me be.

She hurt me bad; the pain is deep,
from all the promises she couldn't keep.
All the lies I heard her say,
are in my head and just won't fade.

How can I forget her, leave her behind?
Erase the memories from my mind?
She doesn't love me, and she never will,
she will never care how I feel.

POEM-67

She stood on the bridge
in silence and fear,
for the demons of darkness
had driven her here.
They cut her heart
right out of her chest,
making her believe
that the demons knew best.
They were always there,
sometimes just out of sight;
waiting in the background,
till the time was right.
These demons were destructive,
knocking down the life she knew,
hating everything about her—
She hated herself too.
These demons can't be seen,
but they're far from fairy tales.
They live inside your mind,
their evilness prevails.
So, on the bridge she stood,
about to end the fight,
then she stopped and thought—
I'll fight them one more night.

POEM-68

Amazing and beautiful,
not a flower or a tree.
Much prettier than that,
and only I can see.

Loving and caring
right down to the core;
filling me with happiness
and so much more.

Eyes are so stunning,
cannot look away.
Gorgeous and shining,
all throughout the day.

Here in your arms
is where I belong.
The beating of your heart
is like a beautiful song.

POEM-69

I love writing poetry,
so the words all rhyme;
it's like music to my ears—
it just takes a little time.

Some are short,
and some are long.
Some people get it right,
and others get it wrong.

But to write a poem,
is to dig down deep,
and search inside yourself,
of things you just can't keep.

Share your love of poetry,
your thoughts and your desires.
Let them burn throughout your soul,
and someday, be admired.

POEM-70

A special place for you and me,
an undying bond to guide us free.
Loneliness blocking the day,
our love lighting the way.

Your gentle touch,
your smiling face.
There is no corner,
no dark place.

Our passion flowing in the waves,
my heart stands still,
awaiting your pace.

Our love with standing time,
diminishing doubt in our mind.
There is no place I'd rather be,
than in your heart and in your dreams.

POEM-71

Come for me, sweet tomorrow,
help me touch the sky;
Like a well-learned bird opens its wings,
I, too, want to fly high.
Don't let the darkness of yesterday
blind my vision to evolve.
Coming out of the bitterness of the past,
help me let my flaws absolve.
Make me like a rainbow,
the colors mingled together,
but all of them in show.
Help me discover my hidden talent,
and pull myself together with efforts gallant.
Let me be a beacon of goodness
for the people I meet.
Help me hear the music of life,
and follow every beat.
Come for me, sweet tomorrow,
help me touch the sky;
like a well learned bird opens its wings,
I, too, want to fly high.

POEM-72

God gave each of us a special family
that we can call our own.
A family that loves us for who we are,
so we would never feel alone.

They may not like everything we do,
or everything we say,
but the beautiful thing about "family"
is that they love us anyway.

Sometimes we feel rejected
by people who do not care,
but our hearts are warmed when remembering
that our family is always there!

So hug them a little more often,
for sometimes we hurt the one we love,
and tell them how much you love them,
for they were sent to you from above.

POEM-73

You are my guiding star,
you are my shining light,
you are my everything,
what helps me through the night.

You are my heart,
you are my soul,
you are my savior,
what makes me feel whole.

You are more than my sister,
you are my best friend,
you are the one who will be there,
when my heart needs to mend.

I love you, sister,
more than you will ever know;
you are my other half.
With you, I am whole.

POEM-74

Sisters are a gift from god,
sisters are your friends.
Sisters stay right by your side
when the road twists and bends.

Sisters never let you down,
they always lend a hand.
Sisters are the best example
of leaving footprint in the sand.

Sisters love girls' night-outs
and painting each other's nails.
They love giving you advice
when everything you've tried fails.

Sisters always love each other,
their love never goes away.
Instead, God makes it grow
stronger every day.

Sisters may have fights sometimes,
but they always stay together.
No matter where your sister goes,
she'll be in your heart forever.

POEM-75

Your birthday is the day I remember
all the wonderful things you do.
Time will fly; each day goes by,
and I've forgotten to say "thank you".

Thank you for teaching me strength
to have confidence while I grow;
for helping me through my biggest challenges;
and for teaching me what I know.

Although our paths may be distant,
and we spend so much time apart,
remember you are the one
who made the essence of my heart.

I will never forget you until my last breath,
this I know for sure,
as you are the first love I ever had,
and so I will love forever more.

POEM-76

I came to visit you today
to place this flag next to your grave;
the sacrifices you have made
will forever be indebted this day.

I came to visit you today
to place this flag next to your grave;
it doesn't matter if you fought or not,
'cause with that uniform it doesn't matter what.

I came to visit you today
to place this flag next to your grave;
the memory of what once was you
still lingers true for those who knew.

I came to visit you today
to place this flag next to your grave;
to just say thank you on this Memorial Day.

POEM-77

It's the season for warmth and cheer,
to be with our family and those we hold dear.
But what if we are miles away?
What if we can't be there on Christmas day?
We could send a beautiful Christmas card,
a glittery ornament that shines like a star,
a tin of cookies so warm and sweet,
but there's only one gift that makes it complete.

It's sent through the snowflakes in the air,
through an angel's peaceful and heavenly prayer,
through the verdant Christmas tree,
through the Holy Babe, sleeping peacefully.
The gift is magical in every way,
it only comes on Christmas day.
It's what makes us truly rich;
a heartfelt, loving Christmas wish.

It's bright and big, like the Bethlehem star,
it stretches wide and travels far.
It's the first snow of Christmas day,
it's the sun's warm and hopeful ray.
This precious gift I gladly send,
it's a Christmas wish to my family and friends:
may love, peace, and joy in your lives stay,
and may you have a merry Christmas always.

POEM-78

An angel from heaven,
who'd been waiting for birth,
is excited to be joining
your family on Earth.

An angel far envied
up there in the blue
when learned its parents
down here would be you.

Baby angels need care,
leaving Father above,
they hope for a family
where there's lots of love.

Where God's light shines brightly
within welcome doors;
A home filled with happiness,
a home just like yours!

POEM-79

Which was brought from the depths of the ocean,
That lamp in a small stream flowing,
why the desire to wake up my mind
or mind is saying to my heart.

Even if I found something
or lose everything has remained the same.
One anecdote reminds me
when I thought he was saying goodbye.

Where was the sun that day,
where the moon that night swept?
Perhaps forcing rain to end,
the desires of my heart flowed.

Well, who knows the heart sigh,
the poor little heart just cries longer.
I do not know the secret of the heart,
what he was saying, everything slat.

The wealth of the world's bodies deal;
hearts were incomplete deal here,
the next moment the sun look now,
the dream remained a dream.

POEM-80

You are just amazing! I know
everyone has bent their head before you.
Where were you born? I don't know.

You are the king! I know
everyone needs you, nothing than you,
Where did you come from? I don't know.

You are just amazing! I know
everyone strives to earn you.
Where did they find you? I don't know.

You are just something! I know
everyone suffers without the presence of you.
Where did you conquer us? I don't know.

You are just everything! I know
everyone forgets anything, if they stand beside you.
Where did you make us mad? I don't know.

How will you find me..!?

POEM-81

O’ father, O’ master of all,
we are children, innocent and small.
Please show us the way, so that we may obey
and attain salvation, O’ lord,
O’ father.

May the world be united and one,
may love prevail and hatred be shunned,
may violence decrease and all live in peace,
with good will may battles be won.
May your message spread through the world,
and bring us all closer to God;
please show us the way.

We get lost in the pleasure of life,
we get shaken when troubles arise
in sorrows, and joy is always nearby
to help us out of our strife.
Be our strength when we become weak,
your guidance and blessings we seek;
please show us the way.

POEM-82

I carry a lighted candle
through a small window
of time, to kindle life within me
nine months later.
As an orange-red sun seeks refuge
in night's embrace,
I travel through my body to reach you.
I live each breath of yours.
You are a face in today's moon,
through winding tributaries
of blood-conduits, I race to keep pace
with the flow of my blood, your blood.
I shiver through contractions
of every muscle in the womb,
their finger movements' coverage
in your tiny being.
Increases of smiling thoughts,
I live a secret dream with you
sharing unspoken words.
I turn the needles of my clock
for dawn to step early,
weaving tomorrow's face;
magic in your first cry,
in answer to the call of the world.
The river of love gushes out, in touching you
I touch the face of god.
As dawn descends this morning, a twin sun rises
alongside the diurnal morning star.

POEM-83

Thou have arrived in all the glory,
with knowledge supreme,
and worlds in a scurry.
Masses are amazed
at your mere glimpse,
their bloated egos make them shrink.
But storm of the truth, so strong and vast,
the ignorance and gloom
can never long last.
Since thou art the path,
and thin is the light,
seeing me in the mirror so bright.
Make me realize the truth eternal,
I've shed the bonds:
worldly, material or parental.
Knowledge of self, who then cares for
power, pomp and pelt.
Perfect master is at the door,
if salvation is your wish
submit yourself at "God's" feet;
there lays the eternal bliss.

POEM-84

I remember those memories,
all peaceful and bright,
the excitement in my emotions
whenever you came in sight.

That royal and glorious shine,
that pure and pious face,
that used to brighten my mood up
in the darkest of my days.
I remember those times
when you used to bless my life
with material and emotional joy,
making me feel truly alive.

That slight mischief in your eyes,
that ever-forgiving personality
that used to embrace every fault in me.
The most comforting version of reality,
there's no positive end to this one,
all I'm doing here is writing in grief,
for the master is still here to love us.
But it's the mother I miss that had to leave.

POEM-85

Knowledge is just like money:
the more we get,
the more we can spend.

It is quite like buckets of water:
the more we store,
the more we can use.

Knowledge is as delicious as tasty food:
the more we taste,
the more we want to take.

It is the key to wisdom,
which opens the lock of the future.

Knowledge brings light in our life
that destroys darkness.
Knowledge is genius,
it is wonderful.
Knowledge is our hero;
Without it…
Everything is zero.

POEM-86

Broken bottles and charred pieces of glass,
wadded-up newspapers tossed on the grass,
pouring of concrete and tearing out trees;
this is environment that surrounds me?

Poisons and insecticides sprayed on our food,
oceans filling with thick oil crude.
All sea life destined to a slow, awful doom;
these are the livings we are to consume?

Mills pumping out iron, expelling yellow fumes,
airlines emitting caustic gases from fuels,
weapons of destruction tested at desolate sites;
and this is the air that's to sustain life?

There has to be something that someone can do,
like raise awareness to those around you,
that if we don't heed the problem at hand—
it's your life that's at stake, make it move.

POEM-87

Here I sit, all alone,
in my quiet, empty home.
Where do broken hearts go
on this sweethearts' day?
I don't know!
Rest assured, I will visit your grave,
grasping our love and the memories we made.

I can't let you go.
I can't make you stay.
So tell me now,
what do I do with this day?

Broken Hearts' day,
that's what today is;
tears and sadness are how I live.
Partners for life, that's what you said,
but here I lie alone in our bed.

So full of sadness, consumed in grey.
No one to hold me on Valentine's Day.
You will be mine again someday,
but for now,
right here where I lay,
all alone on this
Broken Hearts' Day.

POEM-88

I sent a rose to you today,
I hope you didn't mind.
I left it with the Archangel
who was standing just outside.

I left a note upon it,
signed to my valentine.
The simple words were blurred
from the tears I could not hide.

You have enriched my life with laughter
and made the sun to shine.
I love you and I miss you,
signed your valentine.

Sometimes when my heart is heavy,
and these fears I can't avoid,
I would rather have loved you for a moment
than to have an empty void.

Please save a place for me, my love,
I hope you wouldn't mind.
Remember that I love you,
signed your valentine.

POEM-89

Excellence is the habit of perfection.
Not any art a bit shaken;
it's a masterpiece to add peace.
Excellence is the habit of perfection.
It's a building, not a block,
it's a brick, not a rock,
it's a balloon, not a ball;
excellence is the habit of perfection.
It's an exclamation, not a question,
it's the light in the dark,
it's not a fish, but a shark;
excellence is the habit of perfection.
It's a hobby, not a shabby,
to be clean and dirty,
to be neat and dirty;
excellence is the habit of perfection.
To come first and help the worst,
to understand what is the best,
to be sharp by mind and strong by heart;
this is excellence, this is perfection,
this is the habit you need to build.

POEM-90

Whenever I'm around you,
I feel like I'm complete.
I don't know what to say,
but you make my heart beat.
I'm scared to say hello,
but it hurts to say goodbye.
I've been hurt before;
now, I feel love's just a lie.

I'm falling really hard,
there's no stopping me this time.
I think that you're there to catch me,
to finally let me shine.

I lose my voice,
when you're nearby.
I'm scared to mess things up,
I'm scared you'll say good-bye.
I'm sorry if I'm wrong,
when it comes to liking you.
Just tell me know,
I don't want to be hurt by you.

POEM-91

Just for today,
can we forget about race?
Color, religion,
and who isn't straight?

Just for today,
can we forget about soil?
Land, who it belong to,
why do we fight over soil?

Just for today,
can we forget about God?
Who's right or wrong?
Can we spread more love?

Just for today,
let us forget about creed.
No more fighting or hatred,
aren't we just human beings?

POEM-92

I will always be there for you,
I am your little friend;
I will always be in love with you,
all the way till the end.

I will always care for you,
I will never leave.
You're the person
I can never deceive.

I shall go off to sleep
much before you think.
Maybe I'm not with you,
the next second you blink.

The day I'm not with you,
just close your eyes
and take my name.
I promise you dear,
your life will be the same.

I will love you more and more,
with each rising day.
I will always be there for you,
even if we are far away.

POEM-93

If you take me,
take me for who I am.
If you love me,
accept me with all my faults.

If you love me,
don't judge me when I make mistakes,
for I am only human,
and longing to be loved.

If you truly love me,
don't worry about the looks.
Deep within me is a seed of love,
waiting the burst forth.

Love is like a bud:
beautiful, blind and ready to blossom.
Love is like a petal:
poised and pretty as a summer's day.

Embrace the beauty of my heart,
care for the beauty of my soul.
I am who I am,
so, accept me for who I am.

POEM-94

I tried so hard,
I tried my best,
I gave you my all,
and now, there is nothing left.

You stole my heart,
then tore it in two,
now I'm falling apart,
and don't know what to do.

Divided my decisions,
burned by the fire,
confused by your words,
tempted by desire.

I'm living in the present,
my mind is in the past,
not knowing what I'll lose,
not knowing how I'll last.

Blinded by fire,
drowning in doubts,
struggling to be free,
looking for a way out.

READERS NOTE & REMARK

www.ingramcontent.com/pod-product-compliance
Ingram Content Group UK Ltd.
Pitfield, Milton Keynes, MK11 3LW, UK
UKHW021935190726
13853UKWH00004B/1456

9 789354 726798